From Your Village
To
Your
City

By

Silver Nkomane

From your Village to your City

From your Village to your City

With a Foreword

By

Blessed Thabang Mobosi

From your Village to your City

From your Village to your City

Edited and Published by
William Jenkins
4036 Pine Street
Burnaby BC V5G 1Z5 Canada
williamhenryjenkins@gmail.com
http://williamjenkins.ca
Telephone: 1-604-685-4136

ISBN South Africa: Paperback 978-0-620-78532-7
ISBN Canada: Paperback 978-1-928164-41-8
ISBN Canada: Electronic Book 978-1-928164-42-5
Copyright Silver Nkomane © 2018
All rights reserved.

From your Village to your City

Dedication

I Dedicate This To The Youth And The Parents Of Our Present Generation And The Generation To Come.

From your Village to your City

Author

Author Silver Nkomane

My name is Silver Nkomane. I was born on 26 September 1999. I live in South Africa, Greater Tzaneen Municipality in Nkomaneni Dan C Village with my parents, with two sisters and one young brother.

I'm in grade 11 at Progress Secondary School, doing my science subjects. I believe my calling is to become an engineer.

I am mentored by Blessed Thabang Mobosi, a prolific author of a number of books, a great motivator and inspiration to our generation. I am part of his preaching and motivational campaign that is raising great leaders of tomorrow. I am also in his Evangelical Campaign affecting the lives of our youth in our community. We are helping to raise a generation of powerful agents of change who will make Africa a better place tomorrow.

Contact: 0632779305

Email: silver.nkomane@gmail.com

Acknowledgement

I give my thanks to my mentor Blessed Thabang Mobosi. Thank you for taking me from where I was to where I am today. I am because you are, sir.

I give my thanks to my wonderful parents, Mr. William Dingani Nkomane and Mrs. Susan Nkomane. Thanks for your support while raising me into who I am today.

From your Village to your City

Foreword

As a mentor, preacher, motivator, author of number of books including my first book titled "Destiny is a Matter of Choice" as well as a leader of a number of organizations, I recommend this book to you written by my mentee, Silver Nkomane.

It is the duty of each of us to move from where we are to where we are supposed to be. It is an error to remain in your village. We all have a destination to discover; for this purpose many young people have to move from their village to their city.

My mentee, Silver Nkomane, provides guidance on how you can arrive to your destination in life with regard to overcoming every circumstance that might lead to misfortunes. He is someone who grew up in the village and observed many dying in their wilderness not knowing that there is another side of life.

It is not where you come from but where you're going based on the choices you make that Silver identifies. This book will guide you through your steps in moving from your destitution to your destination.

From your Village to your City

Contents

Introduction

I want to thank you for taking the time to read or listen to my views on how we teenagers, living in villages in South Africa, can find our way out of the poverty we inherited and make a successful life for ourselves. Before I begin, I wish to acknowledge that many of these ideas and recommendations are ones I have learned and adopted from the writings and lectures of my mentor, Blessed Thabang Mobosi. His enthusiasm and encouragement point the way for us to follow.

The actions and activities include being close to your family, setting achievable goals for yourself, getting the most education you can absorb, moving from the village to a place where opportunities abound, taking advantage of your talents, planning your future, overcoming temporary setbacks or failures, choosing friends and associates wisely, and being persistent and determined to succeed by making thoughtful, good choices.

I was born into and grew up in a poor family. Many of us who live in South African villages know poverty at first hand. Having been born into a poor family does not mean that I am destined always to be poor. We are probably where we are because of decisions and choices made by our parents and by their parents for as far back in time as we can determine. It does not mean that we must live our lives in poverty and die in the village where we were born. If we don't want that future, we must make choices that will take us out of poverty, perhaps becoming the first member of our family who is financially rich.

1

Many people who are born into a poor family give up on their dreams when they strike the first obstacle. However, being born into a poor family is not an excuse for failure. There is always something that can bring about a change, something that results in a better situation. If you choose to be a thug, steal property or do other illegal activity, you cannot excuse this behavior or your use of drugs or alcohol because of the stress of poverty. You can and should focus on whatever will bring you to a better future.

We might have been born into a poor family, but we don't have to leave ourselves there. We don't have to give up on our dreams because of our background. Life provides many choices. We need to stand up and make the right choices to change our situation.

Family

I have learned to accept what I have and I'm grateful.

Imagine the pain my mother felt when she gave birth to me. When I was sick, she was the one making sure that I survived.

She was there for me all the years until I grew up to be the man that I am today.

There is no love that is more special than the love of family.

These days, because we think we've grown and are adults, we even lay our hands gently on our mother's face. When she speaks with us peacefully, we answer back as if she is our friend. Yes, some of us do this.

When we were young, our mother used to tell us to be home before 5 p.m., but now because we've grown, we come back home whenever it pleases us, even in the morning. If our parents worry every night because of our behavior, we don't know that. They are trying their best to protect us, but we may not appreciate it.

Now is the time to love our parents, support them and show them that we appreciate everything they do for us. Regardless of who is taking care of us, perhaps both our mother and father, we must learn to be grateful.

When our parents stress the value of our education and encourage us to study and stay in school, it is because they see a better future for us than they have been able to achieve. When they tell us to be careful to associate with good people, to treat everyone fairly and decently, to control our sexual desires, to remember our obligations to

3

our church and to use our many talents, they are providing the leadership and guidance that we need.

Coming of Age

The teenage years are our time to change from being a child to being an adult. The process can be quite stressful, particularly if we take ourselves too seriously.

The Opposite Sex

Girls mature earlier than boys so we often find that a 16-year-old boy is attracted to a 14-year-old girl. We usually meet someone new at school and get to know them in the classroom and after school.

Falling in Love

When we find someone we think we love, it is wonderful if the feelings of love are reciprocated. The interest seems to fill our every hour. Nothing else really matters. This is when we have to start to learn to control our actions.

Playing Around

Initially we just "goof" around, trying to attract the other person's attention. Then we meet and talk and talk and talk. Then we make the first overtures of touching, holding hands, walking together.

We engage in different activities, such as going to parties and establish a serious relationship sometimes at the wrong time, with the wrong people and often in the wrong environment.

Kissing, Petting, Sexual Intercourse

If the relationship continues, we try kissing. Feeling braver we try and accept petting. Eventually, we want to go all the

4

way. The question, of course, is: "What should we be doing?"

Teenage pregnancy adds to the poverty in that it often causes a change in the destiny of both parents and a newborn child. Most teenagers between the ages of 14 and 16 are greatly affected.

Most of the young girls who become pregnant have parents who tell them to stay away from boys and concentrate on their studies. Some parents try hard to protect their daughters, try their best to take care of them and give them advice that they know is essential. Some of the girls are ungrateful and do not feel satisfied with the plans their parents have for them. They need to satisfy their pleasures, so they sneak out while their parents are sleeping and find willing boys to explore their sexuality.

When their parents caution them about their deeds and their choices, they disdain advice and decide otherwise. Young boys are equally guilty of ignoring their parents' advice.

I think that most of us who are influenced in this way can be helped if we gain discipline. A poverty mentality and thoughts of being denied life's pleasures lead us to a lack of discipline. It is discipline that leads to success at the end.

It's not that we don't listen when our parents talk to us, but that we think that we are cleverer than our uneducated parents. Instead of deciding to concentrate on our studies so that we can bring a change in our life, we do what we think is best at the time only to find out later what a mistake we have made.

Some girls get into relationships with men or boys who claim that they love them. When they find out later that they were deceived by their lover and blinded by their needs, they find themselves pregnant with no one able or willing to take care of their child.

Usually, the girl has to drop out of school to take care of her child. Stopping her education brings about a significant change in the direction of her destiny. If there is no one to help her, she ends up in poverty, scraping by, blaming everyone but herself. Very often the boy's life is changed as well. His reputation, his integrity and his sense of responsibility are all in question.

A baby needs someone to take care of it. Will it be you, me, your parents or my parents? Both sets of parents were ignored when they were talking about getting an education. Learn to listen to your parents.

Social Diseases

These days, the lack of protection opens the door to getting and spreading diseases, including AIDS. If we do not have the discipline to wait until we are educated and ready for a family before we start having sex, at least we should use protection to avoid getting a deadly disease.

Avoiding Unwanted Pregnancy

We can avoid unwanted pregnancy with modern birth control medicine. However, there are dangers in birth control pills. Some women die from a blood clot caused by the birth control pills. Condoms do break occasionally, resulting in an unexpected and unwanted pregnancy. Aborting a pregnancy is a standard medical procedure, but it would leave me with a feeling of guilt and questions about myself and my partner.

Many a young girl becomes pregnant unintentionally. To avoid having to deal with a pregnancy, I accept what I have and do whatever I can to bring changes in my life in a positive way. I avoid activities that could affect my destiny in a bad way.

Wait for the Right Time

I have decided to wait for the right time, a time when I have completed my education, have my own job, have my own partner and have my own house. Then I can have my own kids. I just don't want to happen to have kids before the right time. I open my textbooks and search for a bright future.

Blessed Thabang Mobosi says **"Not everything that makes you feel good is good, and not everything that is good for others is good for you"**.

It's not about good or what makes you feel good. It's all about doing what is right at the right time with the right person at the right place. Because I do what is best for me, I am in control of my destiny.

Goals

Goals are the results that we aim to achieve in life. They come from our plans. Goals are important because they give us direction by helping us to move from where we are to where we want to be.

I am in charge of my future. In a sense, I am an artist with the pencil in my hand. I draw the kind of future that I'm hoping for.

Goals are personal, unique or special and they describe the results we want to achieve within a certain scale of time.

Short and Long Term Goals

- **Short Term Goals**

These are goals that I aim to achieve in a short period of time such as a week, a month or a few months. They are sometimes considered to be items on a "Things To Do" list.

- **Medium Term Goals**

These goals are ones that can be achieved in one to three years. These goals can include passing certain grades in school, being accepted for a particular course or saving a specific amount of money doing a part-time job.

- **Long term Goals**

These life goals can be achieved in more than 3 years, perhaps as long as 10 years. They could include becoming a specialist in a particular subject, obtaining a university degree, making a particular salary or starting a successful company.

What goals do I have? What I doing to make them a reality?

Well, I intend to finish and pass my secondary school courses. I plan to help others out of poverty by giving talks such as this one and by publishing this book in 2018. In the long term, I plan to start a business providing services to villagers moving to the city.

A dream does not just come to pass through happenstance. Something has to be done in order for a dream to become reality, for things to happen.

The best thing I can do is write down the dream for my life and list the goals that I need to achieve in order to live that dream.

Village Life

Many of the residents in a typical village in South Africa are poor people. The village is a place without electricity, without sufficient food, a place where there is no development. The villagers spend most of their time just existing, getting the food for the next meal, caring for the family members and visiting with others in the same circumstances.

Many of the young girls and boys who have grown up in the villages think their lives will be spent where they are. Their dreams are too small. They think that the village is the only destination for them. Just because they come from a rural village, they do not need to live there all their life. Their lives need not end where they are.

When it comes to school, they often don't even bother to attend. If they do go to school, boys will walk around making noise, smoking and bullying other learners.

As a teenager in a village, I go out and explore so that I can see the gap between what I know and what I do not know. Since I cannot afford to travel, I use the library and the Internet to learn about distant lands and cities. I need to learn more about life. There is much more to life than what I can see in the village. I think about my future and what is to become of me tomorrow. Whatever I see gives me an idea of what I can possess.

Because I am not satisfied with my present situation, I'm doing everything I can to ensure that I'll progress to where I want to be? I'm making choices about my life. These choices are going to bring the future I have planned.

Education

Some teenagers think that life begins and ends in the village where they are born. They compare themselves with people who did not break out of poverty, especially those in their own family. They think that their future is going to be the same as other family members. Therefore, they consider the life changing activities such as education and travel unimportant. They think that education will not bring any change when they consider what it takes to get up the ladder of success so they decide that education is not important in their lives.

Some people drop out of school simply because they can't see the benefit of education. However, education is the key to success. It opens doors for people of all backgrounds. It turns nobody into somebody; it gives the unknown the opportunity to create a way to their fame breakthrough. It is education that replaces an empty mind with an open one.

Many students love sleeping in the classroom during lessons. When there is no teacher in class they just decide not to read or study, but to sleep. The reason they are tired is that they watch TV, use social media, or watch "Whatsapp" until late.

Sleeping in class affects you, the person who is next to you and everybody in the class. If you know you are one of those sleeping in class and you want to improve your marks, you have to listen and pay attention to your teacher. To avoid sleeping in class during lessons you should go to sleep early and stop every unnecessary activity that consumes much of your sleep time.

If you come from a poor background, education is one of the keys that you can use to change your future. Do not despise it because of your origin. It will give you knowledge about the world we live in, offer you the skills you need to survive and provide tools to overcome poverty.

It is education that will take me from where I am to where I want to be. It can take me into the midst of great men and women. It will help me lay a foundation for a successful generation.

Education will help me reach my goals in life. Without it, I will have limited opportunities and other people with education will control my life.

Education is very important in my life. It simplifies my life because it provides a structured set of goals that are achievable. I take it seriously because my success in life depends on it.

Opportunities

An opportunity is a chance for advancement, progress or profit. Many people get an opportunity for something that will help them, but most decline the opportunity. They say, "Now is not the time to act. I'll get another opportunity when I'm better prepared and then I'll go for it". Then the good opportunity is gone.

Good opportunities do not come often. I take every opportunity to attend lectures by Blessed Thabang Mobosi because the ideas and information he provides help keep me motivated to succeed.

There are more opportunities in the larger centres, the towns or cities, than in the village. I may find it necessary to move from the village to a city to find the opportunities that will take advantage of my talents.

There are different means of becoming successful in life. I look for opportunities everywhere and enhance them with a positive mind. If I get an opportunity to do something, I just go for it because I never know if it is the only opportunity I will ever have. I won't be someone who lets opportunity fade away.

There is never a right time or a wrong time. When an opportunity avails itself, it is the right moment to seize it. Many people find themselves in a poor situation that they could have avoided because they did not take the good opportunities they had. I don't look for excuses to turn down an opportunity when it comes; I look for reasons to grab it.

Talents

Most people have a variety of talents, but don't want to reveal them. A talent is a gift, a gift that should be shown to everyone. If I don't display my talent, no one will reveal it for me.

A talent is some ability you have. Your talent can be a motivation to others. You never know how far you can reach if you don't display your talent. Give it a try. One talent that I have is persistence. When I set myself a goal, nothing can stop me from achieving it.

You never know how high you can jump if you don't try to jump. It may be that your future success lies in your talents rather than in getting an advanced education. Not all people who are successful today achieved success through their education. In many cases, it was through using their natural abilities which are talents.

We should do something useful with the talent we have. We should use that talent to encourage others to use theirs. My talent may be the only thing that will put a plate full of good harvest on my table.

Some people chase wrong dreams and copy other people's talents trying to be like them. Some people keep trying to do something they know they'll never be good at, but still they keep on trying. Everybody knows what they are good at and so where their talents lie. We should not be afraid to show our talents to the world.

No one will ever know that your talent is to sing if you only dance and never sing. Let people know that you can do it. Let others be proud of you.

14

Be Curious

Many people are not really curious to know about things that can help them obtain a better future. Some people end up being in situations where they don't know where to go or what to do because they were not curious about the things that would help them in the future.

If you are curious to know about something, ask about it. That's what I do. Getting advice helps me make an informed decision about the path I want to follow. Be the person who likes to know and ask questions. When there is something I don't understand, I get in touch with people who have experience about what I want to know.

Know Who you Are and Where you are Going

Most people in this generation of ours are living without a purpose and without direction as to where their life is navigating. They live a life without meaning; they live as if they are not concerned about anything happening with their life. They are not concerned about life and success, failure and prosperity.

They are like the straw blown by the wind in any direction. They are people without self-discovery, going nowhere; walking, but without a destination to which they are walking. They don't know what they want and where are they going.

Don't be such a person. People with purpose and vision know what they want and where they are going. Everybody has a destination. We choose what we become.

You're here now, but what is to become of you? If you decide to go for something, go for it all out the way I do. Do not give up on the way.

I always know what I want and where I am going. If you know what you want, then you'll know what to do. If you don't know who you are and where you are going, others will choose for you.

If you're not living your life to fulfill your dreams, then you're living your life to help someone else fulfill his or her dreams. Never make the mistake of trying to become what you are not. If you do not know who you are, then choose who you want to be. By simply observing where you come from and making a choice of where you want to go, you can affect what will become of you.

When I observe the lives of many people, I see that many live as though there is no tomorrow. They live their lives as if they do not care about anything. They do bad things trying to make themselves feel good, not realizing that it is doing good things that makes you feel good.

Believe In Yourself

To become successful in life it is not enough for me to utter the desire and find success that occurs the way I said it would. I need to be determined and willing to sacrifice my time and effort to become successful.

Hard work is necessary to reach a destination or goal. I believe in myself; I believe that I will make it regardless of whatever can take place along the road to my destination.

To be successful I need to persist in all that leads to success, with faith, focus and determination. With my persistence it is possible for me to achieve my mission. Faith is the original foundation of determination. If I didn't have it, I couldn't succeed. It doesn't matter what it is that I'm doing or how much interested in it I am, I must believe "I can and I will".

Think of the person who made the first airplane. Nobody believed that such a heavy thing could fly in the sky. I can imagine some people were laughing at him. Those people believed that only birds can fly and said that he was insane.

He believed that he could create something that could accommodate large numbers of people, carry heavy weights and still fly. He went ahead with faith and determination and it happened exactly as he wanted.

In the same way, the people around you might not believe that you can make it to success, but if you can believe in yourself, you can and you will.

Everybody who believes that he or she can make it, will make it.

As one wise man said "If you believe you've won, you've won already, but if you think you'll lost, you've already lost".

Action begins with faith. Intentions without actions are worthless, like a pen without ink. What will you do with a pen without ink?

Therefore, we should always make the effort to break through, to walk to the other side, to accomplish our goals.

Some people say that they no longer believe in their abilities and have no hope for a good future. Not me! I am strong and cannot be discouraged. I have faith and expect to find new opportunities in the future. I believe in myself.

Be Humble and Be Yourself

Many people are not content with who they are. Never try to be someone you're not, just be yourself. Trying to be someone you are not is like trying to repair a glass with plastic. Love who you are and live what you are.

Some people do not achieve great things in life because they are trying to be someone they are not. You could miss being a millionaire because of trying to be a taxi driver. You could buy a car that costs too much money because your neighbors have fancy cars. You'll be poor and die in debt because of trying to be someone you are not from lack of contentment and extravagance.

It is pride that makes people buy expensive things that are not essential. In most cases, you buy on credit, which is not good. Be content with what you have. **"Success is not about having the whole world in your hands; it's about trying to do what you can to be successful at your maximum level without being extravagant,"** says Blessed Thabang Mobosi.

I won't allow life's hurdles to change me from who I am. I do not allow the situation to change me. Rather, I change the situation instead of letting it change me.

Situations do not last for a lifetime, so I do not let every temporary thing in my life change who I am. I do not let influences turn me into making bad choices that will affect me for the rest of my life.

Don't Give Up

The harder it gets every day, the closer we are to success. When we start something, we never give up until we finish it. If we are thinking of giving up, first we ask "Why did I start this in the first place?"

Why should we give up now that we have scars and have handled the pain? We're already in pain and everyone can see our scars. Let them see the results. The more pain we feel, the closer we are to success. No gain without pain.

Always know that "Success follows the hand of the diligent".

Build Your Future

In this world, life becomes tough when you don't build up your future. Always remember that the future will be better than the present. Start to plan and build your future while you are young and still going to school.

I spend most of my spare time reading books not toying with Facebook. I don't spend most of my spare time that I can use to accomplish success doing things that are not beneficial.

I focus on working on my expected achievements.

If you want to build your future, don't move around too much, don't talk too much. If you are always talking, you may lose focus on planning for your future.

If you're a person who is always distracted with social media, find a way to manage so that it doesn't distract you from spending your time on the attainment of your goals.

I let my inner compass guide the decisions I make to build my future. When the voice inside is louder than voices outside, I have begun to master my life. I have developed a strong sense of who I am and I focus on building a life that gracefully aligns with that. What I always remind myself as I build my future is that my individuality is what makes me different. It is what makes me effective.

Planning for my future is a first priority in my life. Everything else can be addressed later. As they say, if you fail to plan you have already planned to fail.

Why People Give up in Planning Their Future

Most people on a mission of building their future end up giving up in the planning. You might hear about someone who gave up his dreams not because of someone, but because of himself.

When you are on a mission of planning your future or doing something you ought to achieve, you have to watch what you do and watch what you see. What you do or see could make you give up or lose focus or interest in your planning.

Planning needs more focus and more time. It needs sacrifices because you will have to leave some other things in order to achieve your planning.

Some people give up in achieving their future because they chose wrong directions and ended up becoming something they never intended to be. You're what you say you are, and you're what you repeatedly do. You're going to be wherever you're going to be not because of anyone, but because of what you choose to do. These choices lead you to your destiny.

Disappointments

Everybody can get disappointed in life by family, friends, siblings, teachers, at work, by their beloved ones and others. You can be disappointed by anybody, even people you trust the most. You can look for a job and be disappointed by not being accepted. Some people give up on everything when they get disappointed in life. Disappointment is similar to failure. I handle failure by believing that I will make it in the next round.

If I fail I don't give up. I stand up and believe that although I once failed, I won't fail again. Just as when I face a disappointment in life, I take disappointment and failure as tests of how strong I am. They make me know that there is still hope. I believe if a door closes against me in life, another one is certainly opening.

I don't let a disappointment define me as a failure. I don't let it discourage me or make me want to give up on something I wish to achieve. I refuse to let a disappointment define me as a weak person. I have new hope in myself and knowledge that I will never give up. By being confident in myself I can overcome any disappointment or failure.

Alone You Can Do It

Once upon a time there was a young boy who had two friends. This boy was a dreamer. He used to dream big and aim high, aiming higher than his friends. He really wanted to be a successful young man. He was very dedicated to his work, really hard-working and determined.

His friends realized that this boy was different from them. They thought he wouldn't be successful without them. Since they were his only friends, they decided to depart from him thinking "He won't make it without us".

When the boys decided to depart from him, he was distressed. He didn't know what to do and who could help or support him. He tried to look for new friends and people who could support him, but he didn't find any. Then he told himself that he could do it alone and he would.

The boy finally made it to success. He made it without any helper or supporter.

Sometimes in life you don't need a friend or anyone in your life to make it to success. You can do it alone even though friends turn their backs on you or depart from you.

If they depart from you, let them go; you can succeed without them. Be like the young boy who told himself that he could and ended up achieving his goals. Never lose confidence.

Those Who Once Failed In Life

The fact that you have once failed in life doesn't mean that you're forever a failure. Failure makes us learn new things and gain new experiences about life. It makes us realize what we do not know. Failure is not fatal and failing can tell you to try again, to try again with a greater effort.

Other people are looking at you since your actions become their motivation. If you give up, they will also give up. It is acceptable to admit your failure. I have done that and it simply provided me with the determination to succeed next time.

Before considering giving up, think of your destiny, think of the people who believe in you, the people who have faith in you and the people who want to learn something from you. Think of how many people you may disappoint or let down. Think about the consequences of giving up. Don't give up.

Your destiny is important to the universe.

I decided to write this book because I also once failed in life. I didn't give up, I stood up and started to believe in myself. I believed that I could try again and I thought of writing this message to you.

Now I'm saying to you: believe in yourself. It doesn't matter how many times you've failed; what matters is what you want to achieve in life. How long it is going to take you to get there doesn't matter; what matters most is getting there.

Never give up hope and patience. Don't be disappointed. Be strong and believe in yourself. The fact that you are in the same battlefield fighting the same battle proves that you are not a failure. You will become a failure only when you stop trying.

Surround Yourself with Successful People

If you want to be successful in life, surround yourself with successful people. A blind man cannot lead another blind man or else they will both fall into a pit.

Many of those who are successful in life surrounded themselves with successful people. That is why they became successful too.

Sometimes it takes only the people who have the same dreams as you to make your dreams come true. The forces that are surrounding you are the ones that will influence you the most.

Sometimes if you want to be successful, you can surround yourself with people who are not yet successful, those who have the same goals as you and are living the life that leads to a successful life; those who are determined and dedicated to their goals.

Have your own goals. Learn to set your goals straight, goals that lead to your desired destination.

Learn to be like successful people; know the secret that leads to their success. When they sacrifice their time, you do the same. If you really want to be successful, sacrifice. It is not an easy thing to do; success comes from hard work.

When I talk about people who sacrifice, I am talking about those who don't care about the condition of the weather. Whether it is cold or hot, they always do what they know will help them in the future.

These people take fewer hours to sleep. They spend many hours working on what they want to achieve in life. That is sacrifice.

Procrastination is a time murderer. Do not waste your time on those things that are non-beneficial and non-essential. Try to be in charge of your time and not your time in charge of you. It is time to kiss your excuses goodbye and begin to do something positive that will move you towards your goals and dreams.

Yes! You can. I believe in you. If you want to be successful in life, apply the principles of sacrifice. No sacrifice means no success.

Make your Choices and your Choices will Make You

Most of the time when we make choices, we don't think of the consequences that are to follow. Remember that the choices that we make in life will determine our future and what will become of us. In every activity, the result will be according to the choices that were made.

If you decide to steal some property and sell it so that you can get money to buy something to eat, you may get away with it several times, but one day you can expect to be in court.

Sometimes you'll hear someone saying "I will kill that person because I don't have a choice". Remember, to kill is a choice with bad consequences, one that you will regret. You might kill and walk free, but one day you'll pay the price as every choice has its own price. You might be the victor today, but tomorrow you'll be the victim.

You'll hear someone saying: "I don't have a choice. I have to do it", because of this and that. Is that an excuse? Remember. Every person has a choice to make. Irrespective of what situation you are in, you can make a positive or negative choice in that moment. Going to school is a choice. It's a choice that will help you to build your future.

Your choices reflect your intentions. You choose whether or not you go to school, believe in a religion, make an honest living, and so much more. Your personal choices lead to your personal consequences. For example, if you choose not to go to school, you don't receive an education, you can't get a decent job or career and you face poverty the rest of your life.

If you decide to be a bad person, it's a choice you make. It's a choice that will make people hate you. If you decide to be a businessman, it's a choice. If you decide to be a good man, it's a choice. It's a choice that will make people love you.

So everything you decide to do is a choice and every choice has its bad and good side to it. The choices we make guide our lives and shape us into the person we choose to be. We control our own lives. No one can make our decisions for us. The ultimate choice of how to live our lives lies within us. We control our own fate.

Learn to make your choices right and your choices will yield the right result. If you make your choices wrong, then your choices will yield wrong results. Therefore, be a responsible, accountable, answerable person.

Friends Are More Influential Than Parents.

Many people usually get bad advice simply because they request it from the wrong people.

Friendly Enemies

Friendly enemies are those who are close to you, who may even be your best friends, but who try to lead you from the path you are following. These people may encourage you to do wrong things that happen to make you feel good. Remember not everything that makes you feel good is good.

Friendly enemies will never tell you that what you are doing is wrong even if it is. They will not encourage you to do anything good. Mostly they pretend to be grateful to be your friend, but they are jealous and they envy you. Their mission is to influence you to do things that will end up destroying your life.

They lead you to do things that could terminate your life or destiny. They try to change your purpose and give you a negative one. They try to change your direction to one that leads to destruction.

Remember friends can be more influential than your parents, your spouse or your mentor.

Who are your friends? Show me your friends and I will tell you who you are by judging their character.

Bad Company

The Bible says "Bad company corrupts good manners".

The people with whom you live can determine what you become in life. The ones who are closest to you and are effective in giving you advice can control your destiny. Students generally spend more time with their friends than with family members or religious leaders.

They say, "Birds of a feather flock together."

They say, "Influence them before they influence you, and do unto them before they do unto you,"

In life you have to watch the kind of company that you keep. Do your friends influence you negatively or positively? Do they give directions that lead to more success in life?

If you associate with people who are not concerned about life and prosperity, but simply drift as the whim takes them one way or another, you will become like them. If you decide to be close to those who perform well in school, you are bound to do well yourself.

Some people are bad. They live without a purpose and they are going nowhere in life. If you live with them, they will kill your vision also. Separate yourself from bad company or they will corrupt your life.

Have you ever heard someone saying "I hate myself"?

I hope you don't want to be in that situation by not making a right choice on the company you keep.

Watch the Company You Keep

The company you keep might change who you are. When you live with Christians, you'll become a Christian. When you live with thugs, you'll become a thug. When you live with drug dealers, you'll become a drug dealer. When you live with people who drink alcohol too much and smoke, you'll become like them. You always end up fitting in with the company you keep.

I am now a motivator because I stayed in the company of my mentor who is always motivating people to shine forth. I am shining because I stay in his shining company. Staying under his shadow has made me to have great expectation for life and the future and to plan in reaching great heights. That young man, Blessed Thabang Mobosi, really inspires me.

Living with people who don't have dreams or goals will cause your own dream to be suppressed. If you live with people who don't like going to school, you'll become like them. The company you keep makes you agree with everything they do. Make sure your friends are not a company of destiny destroyers.

Don't be with people who do bad things because when you do a bad thing you'll pay a price for it.

Watch Who Gives You Advice

People will give you different advice. Some will give you good advice, but some will advise you out of envy. Beware of people who will talk you out of following your golden road.

There are people who you trust and love thinking maybe they trust and love you as well, but they actually don't like you anymore. Such people are hard to identify because they make themselves your friends, but feed you with what turns out to be poisonous advice.

If someone encourages you to do bad things or gives you bad advice, don't show them that you can see what they are up to. Just listen only for that moment. When you walk away, forget the advice and do not spend any more time with them. Such people are dangerous. Some advice seems to be good and reasonable, but comes with a bad outcome when put into practice.

Two Types of People in your Life

There are two types of people in your life: wasters and investors.

Wasters come into your life just to destroy you and everything you've earned and make it become wasted. They are there not to increase you, but to decrease you. They don't have any good thing to do with you. They want to destroy everything you've earned. They want to cause you a pain of loss in your life. If you come across such people in your life, get rid of them. It is better for you to have nobody in your life than to be with wasters. Wasters will kill your joy, passion, dreams, faith and success. You'll never achieve anything in life while still associating with wasters.

When investors come into your life, things will begin to change. If a person knows you as a loser, they'll transform you into a winner. These are people like your mentors and advisers. Everything you touch will be blessed when investors invade your life. These people cause your life to explode in achievements. Keep these people in your life. They come not to decrease you, but to increase you and your visions. They are there to give you hope, increase your faith, make you more positive, and always to help you achieve your goals and reach your dream world.

They are there to take you from your village to your city, the city of your dreams. They help in accelerating your life forward by simply investing in your life.

Who do you associate with in your life, waster or investors?

Three Types of People

Those who Wish for Success

Among those who wish for success are people who like wishing to have what others have. If some neighbour bought a car they'll wish they could buy a car too, but they don't do anything that could make them afford a car. Many who wish for success are people with big dreams, but who don't do anything that could make their dreams a reality. You will hear them saying that in the future they want to drive an expensive car and build a big house, but they don't seem to be working to achieve that wish.

Those Who Wait For Success

Those who wait for success to come to them without working for it should be working on their goals instead of remaining in the same spot.

They expect success to come to them whilst doing nothing. Success follows those who work for it, not those who wait for it.

Those Who Work For Success

Those who work for success are people who know what they want. They set their goals and work hard on achieving them. They know success doesn't come easily, but needs work. They don't wish for success nor wait for success to come to them; they work for it.

If you want to be successful you need to set your goals, have a big mindset and work towards your goals. Focus only on what could lead you to success. Hard work leads to success. Make your wishes and dreams come true by working hard to make them come true. Think, wish and dream and do what leads you to success.

Learn to Subtract Some People from your Life

Sometimes when you're doing something that leads to success, some people will try to distract you. Enemies of success distract you from being successful in life. You should learn to subtract those people from your life when you notice them. Enemies of success are those people who come into your life only to stop you from being successful.

Some of them might be your closest friends. Enemies of success doesn't shout that "I am the enemy of success", but they act as though they are a friend of yours, destroying you slowly until you become like them, people who have no goals, dreams, visions and no future.

Learn to subtract every person who distracts and those who want you to fail and not succeed. If you do not subtract them, they will destroy your plans for a successful life. Subtraction is needed in real life, when we want to be successful. Add friends only when they are needed and are the right people.

Motivated by the Smoke of the Fire

One day I was sitting under a tree when my neighbor was burning papers in her yard. I was really motivated by the smoke of those papers. The smoke was moving upwards. It never moved left or right only always upwards.

It doesn't matter the condition of the weather, whether it's sunny, rainy, windy or cold. You, as a child of destiny, as a person who has goals, as someone really determined to succeed and fully concentrating on your success, succeed in spite of attempts to move you off your course.

Make sure that when storms strike you with destiny destroyers left and right, when betrayers strike, when family abandons you and no longer show support for you, stand firm and walk straight ahead. Never be blown in another direction by the wind.

What do you do when storms of life give you hard time, when the wind blows with pressure to a direction opposite to the one you're following? What do you do? Do you give up or do you go to the direction the wind blows?

Stand up and walk away from your village to your city.

Shalom!

I hope to see you in the city where we will meet and enjoy our success.

Editor

Mr. William Jenkins was born in Ottawa, Canada in 1932. He became a computer programmer and worked in that field for 45 years. Subsequently, he sold residential real estate and then wrote and published a few mystery stories for middle-school children.

After finding publishing using Createspace particularly easy, he began publishing books for others as a free service. There is no charge for the publishing and editing service. See his website

http://williamjenkins.ca

He is especially interested in publishing stories and poems from students. A few students from South Africa have submitted their writing.

If you are a teacher or student, submit your writing to

williamhenryjenkins@gmail.com

From your Village to your City

www.ingramcontent.com/pod-product-compliance
Lightning Source LLC
Chambersburg PA
CBHW061754040426

42447CB00011B/2303